The Easy Vegan Keto Diet Recipes

Fast and Easy Recipes for Your Everyday Meals

Karen Yosco

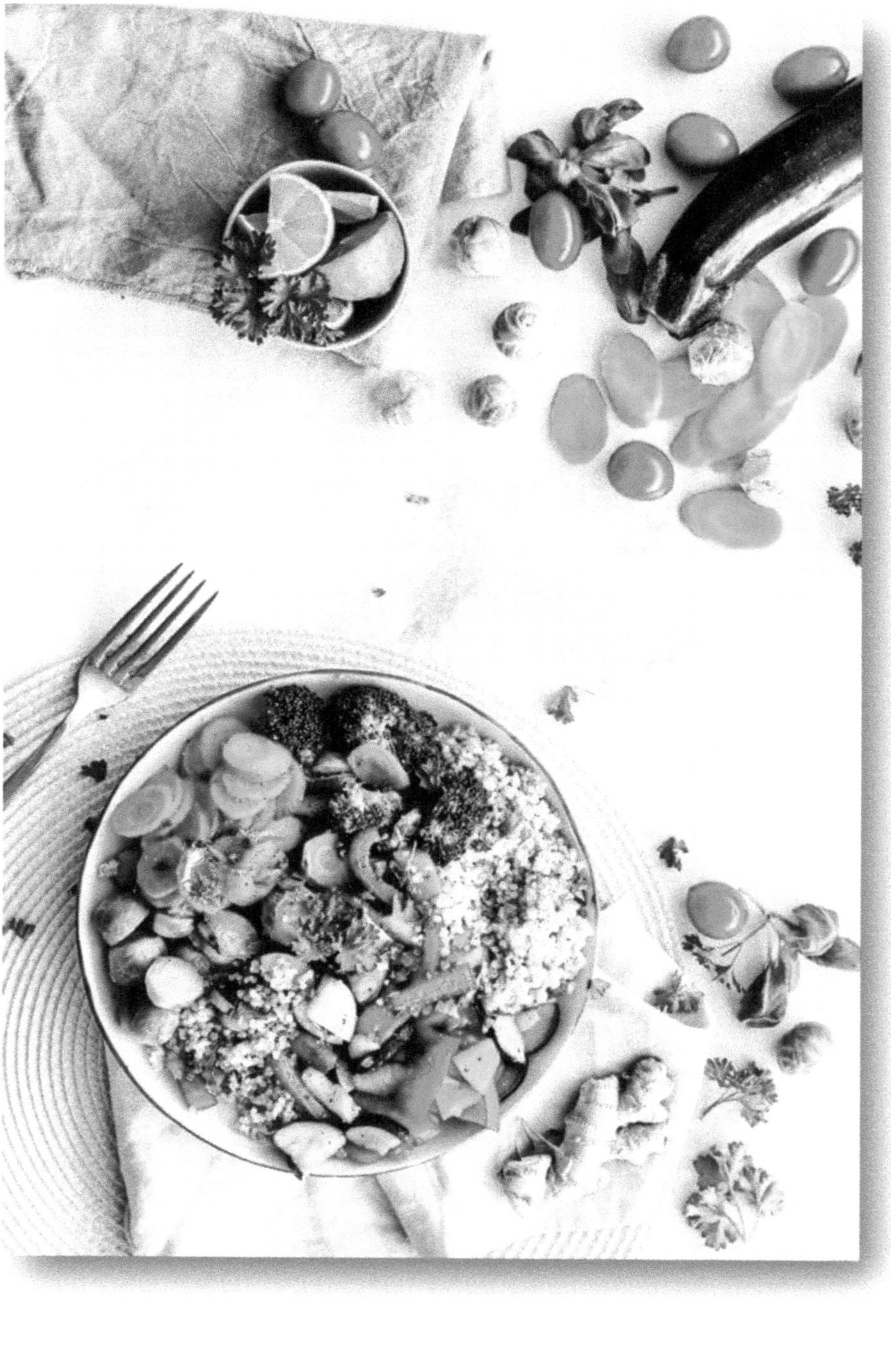

indirect, which are incurred as a result of the use of information contained within this document, including, but not limited to, — errors, omissions, or inaccuracies.

Table of Contents

BREAKFAST

Mint Chocolate Protein Smoothie

Preparation Time: 5 minutes

Cooking Time: 0 minutes

Servings: 4

Ingredients:

- 4 tablespoons ground flaxseed

- 4 cups fresh spinach

- 4 frozen banana, sliced

- 4 scoops of chocolate protein powder

- 4 tablespoons chopped dark chocolate, vegan

- ½ cup melted dark chocolate

- 1 teaspoon peppermint extract, unsweetened

- 4 tablespoons honey

- 3 cups almond milk, unsweetened

- 1 cup ice cubed

Directions:

1. Add all the ingredients in the order into a food processor or blender and then pulse for 1 to 2 minutes until blended, scraping the sides of the container frequently.

2. Distribute the smoothie among glasses and then serve.

Nutrition: 480.5 Cal 20.3 g Fat 8.4 g Saturated Fat 45.6 g Carbohydrates 9.7 g Fiber 22.5 g Sugars 31.2 g Protein

Sunrise Smoothie

Preparation Time: 5 minutes

Cooking Time: 0 minutes

Servings: 4

Ingredients:

- 4 tablespoons chia seed

- 2 frozen banana

- 2 lemon, peeled

- 2 cups diced carrots

- 4 clementine, peeled

- 4 cups frozen strawberries, unsweetened

- 12 tablespoons pomegranate tendrils

- 2 cup almond milk, unsweetened

Directions:

1. Add all the ingredients in the order into a food processor or blender and then pulse for 1 to 2 minutes until blended, scraping the sides of the container frequently.

2. Distribute the smoothie among glasses and then serve.

Nutrition: 274 Cal 5.4 g Fat 0.5 g Saturated Fat 57.3 g Carbohydrates 13.3 g Fiber 33.8 g Sugars 0.5 g Protein

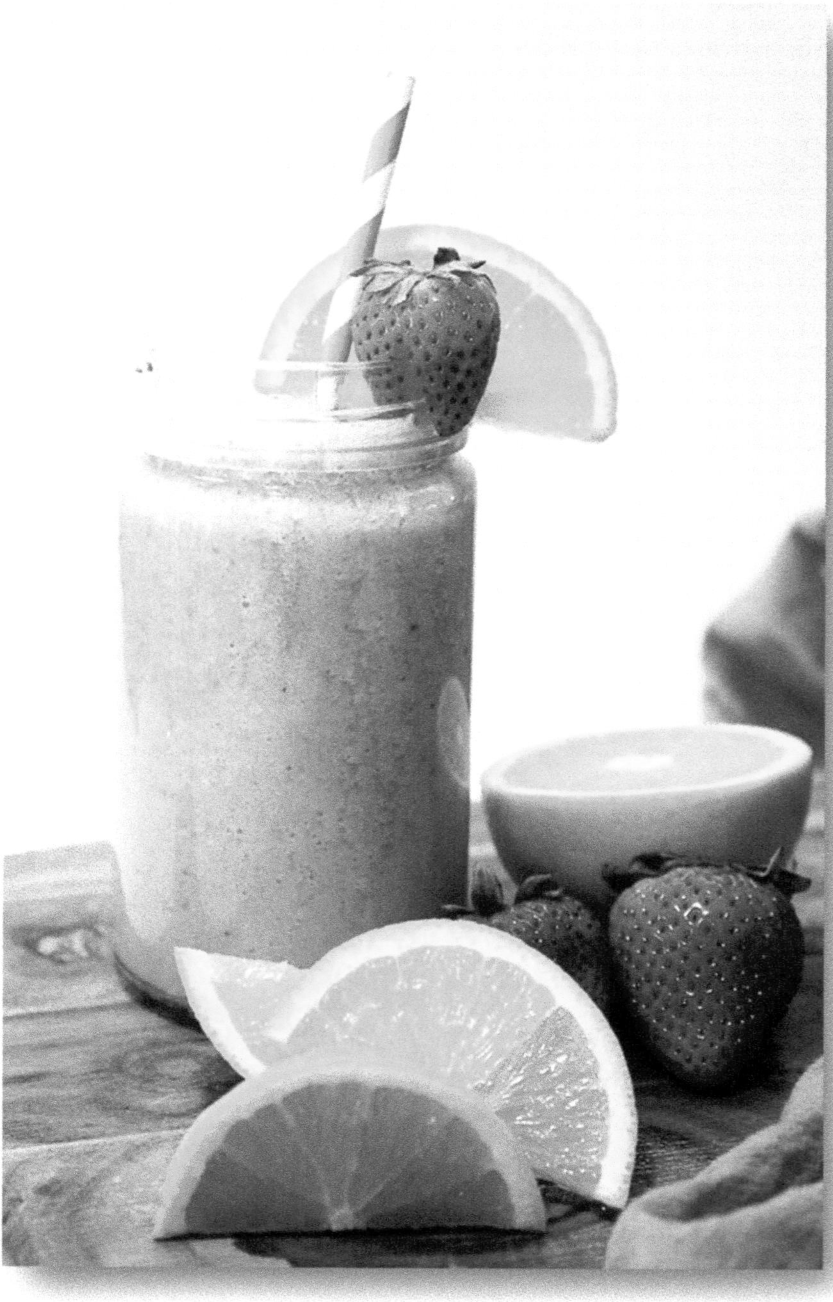

Sunshine Orange Smoothie

Preparation Time: 5 minutes

Cooking Time: 0 minutes

Servings: 4

Ingredients:

- 2 medium oranges, zested, juiced

- 4 frozen bananas

- 4 tablespoons goji berries

- ½ cup hemp seeds

- 1 teaspoon grated ginger

- 1 cup almond milk, unsweetened

- ½ cup of ice cubes

Directions:

1. Add all the ingredients in the order into a food processor or blender and then pulse for 1 to 2 minutes until blended, scraping the sides of the container frequently.

2. Distribute the smoothie among glasses and then serve.

Nutrition: 131 Cal 2.3 g Fat 0.3 g Saturated Fat 26.7 g Carbohydrates 4.4 g Fiber 11 g Sugars 2.6 g Protein

LUNCH

Sabich Sandwich

Preparation Time: 10 minutes

Cooking Time: 10 minutes

Servings: 4

Ingredients:

- 1/2 cup cooked white beans

- 2 medium potatoes, peeled, boiled, ½-inch thick sliced

- 1 medium eggplant, destemmed, ½-inch cubed

- 4 dill pickles, ¼-inch thick sliced

- ¼ teaspoon of sea salt

- 2 tablespoons olive oil

- 1/4 teaspoon harissa paste

- 1/2 cup hummus

- 1 tablespoon mayonnaise

- 4 pita bread pockets

- 1/2 cup tabbouleh salad

Directions:

1. Take a small frying pan, place it over medium-low heat, add oil and wait until it gets hot.

2. Season eggplant pieces with salt, add to the hot frying pan and cook for 8 minutes until softened, and when done, remove the pan from heat.

3. Take a small bowl, place white beans in it, add harissa paste and mayonnaise and then stir until combined.

4. Assemble the sandwich and for this, place pita bread on clean working space, smear generously with hummus, then cover half of each pita bread with potato slices and top with a dill pickle slices.

5. Spoon 2 tablespoons of white bean mixture on each dill pickle, top with 3 tablespoons of cooked eggplant pieces and 2 tablespoons of tabbouleh salad and then cover the filling with the other half of pita bread.

6. Serve straight away.

Nutrition: 386 Cal 13 g Fat 2 g Saturated Fat 56 g Carbohydrates 7 g Fiber 3 g Sugars 12 g Protein

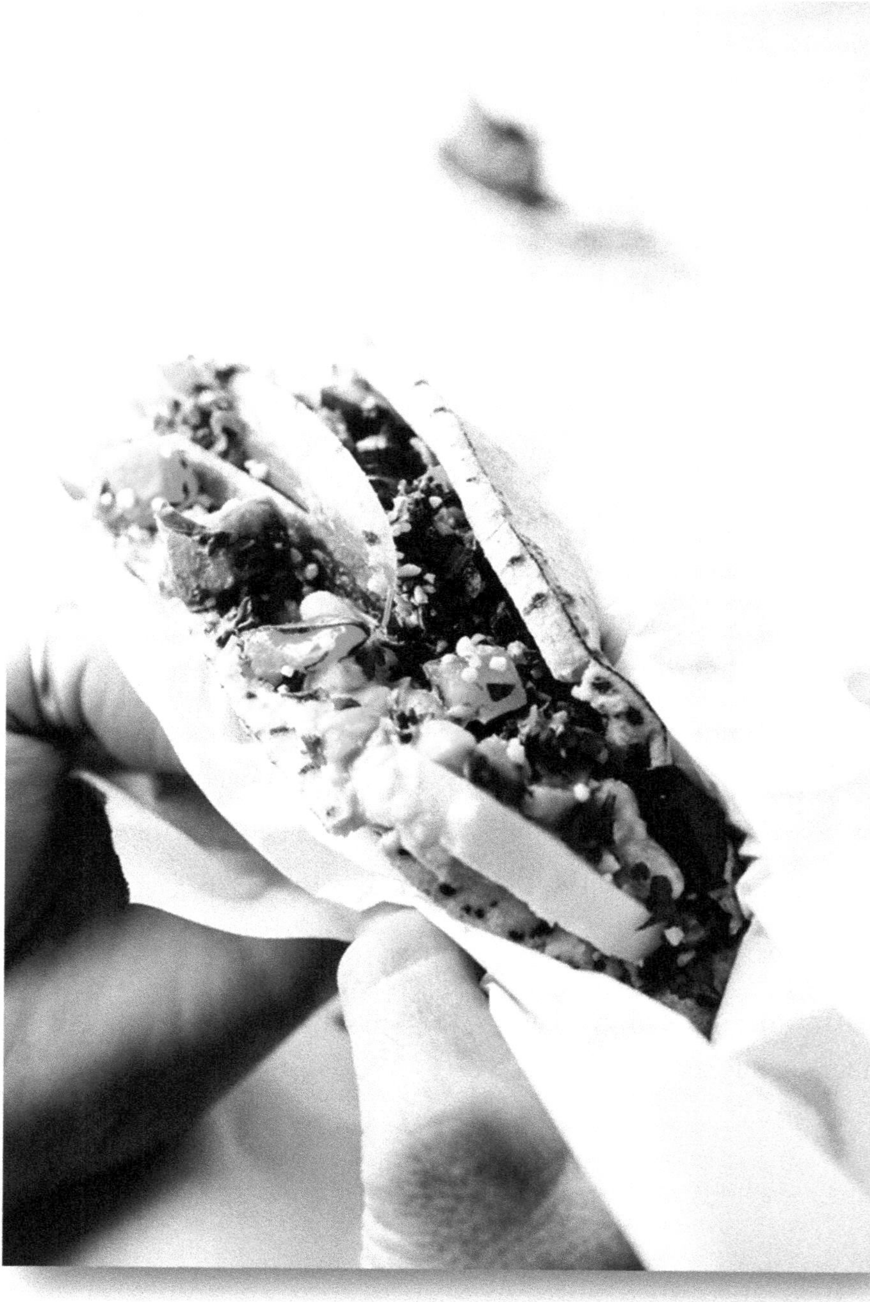

Chickpea and Mayonnaise Salad Sandwich

Preparation Time: 10 minutes

Cooking Time: 0 minutes

Servings: 4

Ingredients:

For the mayonnaise:

- 1/3 cup cashew nuts, soaked in boiling water for 10 minutes

- ½ teaspoon ground black pepper

- 1 teaspoon salt

- 6 teaspoons apple cider vinegar

- 2 teaspoon maple syrup

- 1/2 teaspoon Dijon mustard

For the chickpea salad:

- 1 small bunch of chives, chopped

- 1 ½ cup sweetcorn

- 3 cups cooked chickpeas

To serve:

- 4 sandwich bread

- 4 leaves of lettuce

- ½ cup chopped cherry tomatoes

Directions:

1. Prepare the mayonnaise and for this, place all of its ingredients in a food processor and then pulse for 2 minutes until smooth, scraping the sides of the container frequently.

2. Take a medium bowl, place chickpeas in it, and then mash by using a fork until broken.

3. Add chives and corn, stir until mixed, then add mayonnaise and stir until well combined.

4. Assemble the sandwich and for this, stuff sandwich bread with chickpea salad, top each sandwich with a lettuce leaf, and ¼ cup of chopped tomatoes and then serve.

Nutrition: 387 Cal 19 g Fat 5 g Saturated Fat 39.7 g Carbohydrates 7.2 g Fiber 4.6 g Sugars 10 g Protein

Cheesy Macaroni with Broccoli

Preparation Time: 10 minutes

Cooking Time: 25 minutes

Servings: 6

Ingredients

- 1/3 cup melted coconut oil

- ¼ cup nutritional yeast

- 1 tablespoon tomato paste

- 1 tablespoon dried mustard

- 2 garlic cloves, minced

- 1 ½ teaspoons salt

- ½ teaspoon ground turmeric

- 4 ½ cups almond milk

- 3 cups cauliflower florets, chopped

- 1 cup raw cashews, chopped

- 1 lb. shell pasta

- 1 tablespoon white vinegar

- 3 cups broccoli florets

Directions:

1. Place a suitably-sized saucepan over medium heat and add coconut oil.

2. Stir in mustard, yeast, garlic, salt, tomato paste, and turmeric.

3. Cook for 1 minute then add almond milk, cashews, and cauliflower florets.

4. Continue cooking for 20 minutes on a simmer.

5. Transfer the cauliflower mixture to a blender jug then blend until smooth.

6. Stir in vinegar and blend until creamy.

7. Fill a suitably-sized pot with salted water and bring it to a boil on high heat.

8. Add pasta to the boiling water.

9. Place a steamer basket over the boiling water and add broccoli to the basket.

10. Cook until the pasta is al dente. Drain and rinse the pasta and transfer the broccoli to a bowl.

11. Add the cooked pasta to the cauliflower-cashews sauce.

12. Toss in broccoli florets, salt, and black pepper.

13. Mix well then serve.

Nutrition: Calories: 40; Fat: 2.0g Protein: 5g Carbohydrates: 7g
Fiber: 4g Sugar: 3g Sodium: 18mg

DINNER

Minted Peas

Preparation Time: 5 minutes

Cooking Time: 5 minutes

Servings: 4

Ingredients:

- 1 tablespoon olive oil

- 4 cups peas, fresh or frozen (not canned)

- ½ teaspoon sea salt

- freshly ground black pepper

- 3 tablespoons chopped fresh mint

Directions:

1. In a large sauté pan, heat the olive oil over medium-high heat until hot. Add the peas and cook, about 5 minutes.

2. Remove the pan from heat. Stir in the salt, season with pepper, and stir in the mint.

3. Serve hot.

Nutrition: Calories: 77Fat: 3gProtein: 4gCarbohydrates: 12gFiber: 5gSugar: 3gSodium: 320mg

Glazed Curried Carrots

Preparation Time: 5 minutes

Cooking Time: 15 minutes

Servings: 6

Ingredients:

- 1-pound carrots, peeled and thinly sliced

- 2 tablespoons olive oil

- 2 tablespoons curry powder

- 2 tablespoons pure maple syrup

- juice of ½ lemon

- sea salt

- freshly ground black pepper

Directions:

1. Place the carrots in a large pot and cover with water. Cook on medium-high heat until tender, about 10 minutes. Drain the carrots and return them to the pan over medium-low heat.

2. Stir in the olive oil, curry powder, maple syrup, and lemon juice. Cook, stirring constantly, until the liquid reduces,

about 5 minutes. Season with salt and pepper and serve immediately.

Nutrition: Calories: 171Fat: 3gProtein: 4gCarbohydrates: 34gFiber: 5gSugar: 3gSodium: 129mg

Thai Roasted Broccoli

Preparation Time: 5 minutes

Cooking Time: 15 minutes

Servings: 4

Ingredients:

- 1 head broccoli, cut into florets

- 2 tablespoons olive oil

- 1 tablespoon soy sauce or gluten-free tamari

Directions:

1. Preheat the oven to 425°F. Line a baking sheet with parchment paper. In a large bowl, combine the broccoli, oil, and soy sauce. Toss well to combine.

2. Spread the broccoli on the prepared baking sheet. Roast for 10 minutes.

3. Toss the broccoli with a spatula and roast for an additional 5 minutes, or until the edges of the florets begin to brown.

Nutrition: Calories: 44Fat: 2gProtein: 3gCarbohydrates: 7gFiber: 2gSugar: 3gSodium: 20mg

Coconut Curry Noodle

Preparation Time: 10 minutes

Cooking Time: 30 minutes

Servings: 4

Ingredients:

- ½ tablespoon oil
- 3 garlic cloves, minced
- 2 tablespoons lemongrass, minced
- 1 tablespoon fresh ginger, grated
- 2 tablespoons red curry paste
- 1 (14 oz.) can coconut milk
- 1 tablespoon brown sugar
- 2 tablespoons soy sauce
- 2 tablespoons fresh lime juice
- 1 tablespoon hot chili paste
- 12 oz. linguine
- 2 cups broccoli florets
- 1 cup carrots, shredded

- 1 cup edamame, shelled

- 1 red bell pepper, sliced

Directions:

1. Fill a suitably-sized pot with salted water and boil it on high heat.

2. Add pasta to the boiling water and cook until it is al dente then rinse under cold water.

3. Now place a medium-sized saucepan over medium heat and add oil.

4. Stir in ginger, garlic, and lemongrass, then sauté for 30 seconds.

5. Add coconut milk, soy sauce, curry paste, brown sugar, chili paste, and lime juice.

6. Stir this curry mixture for 10 minutes, or until it thickens.

7. Toss in carrots, broccoli, edamame, bell pepper, and cooked pasta.

8. Mix well, then serve warm.

Nutrition: Calories: 44Fat: 2gProtein: 3gCarbohydrates: 7gFiber: 2gSugar: 3gSodium: 20mg

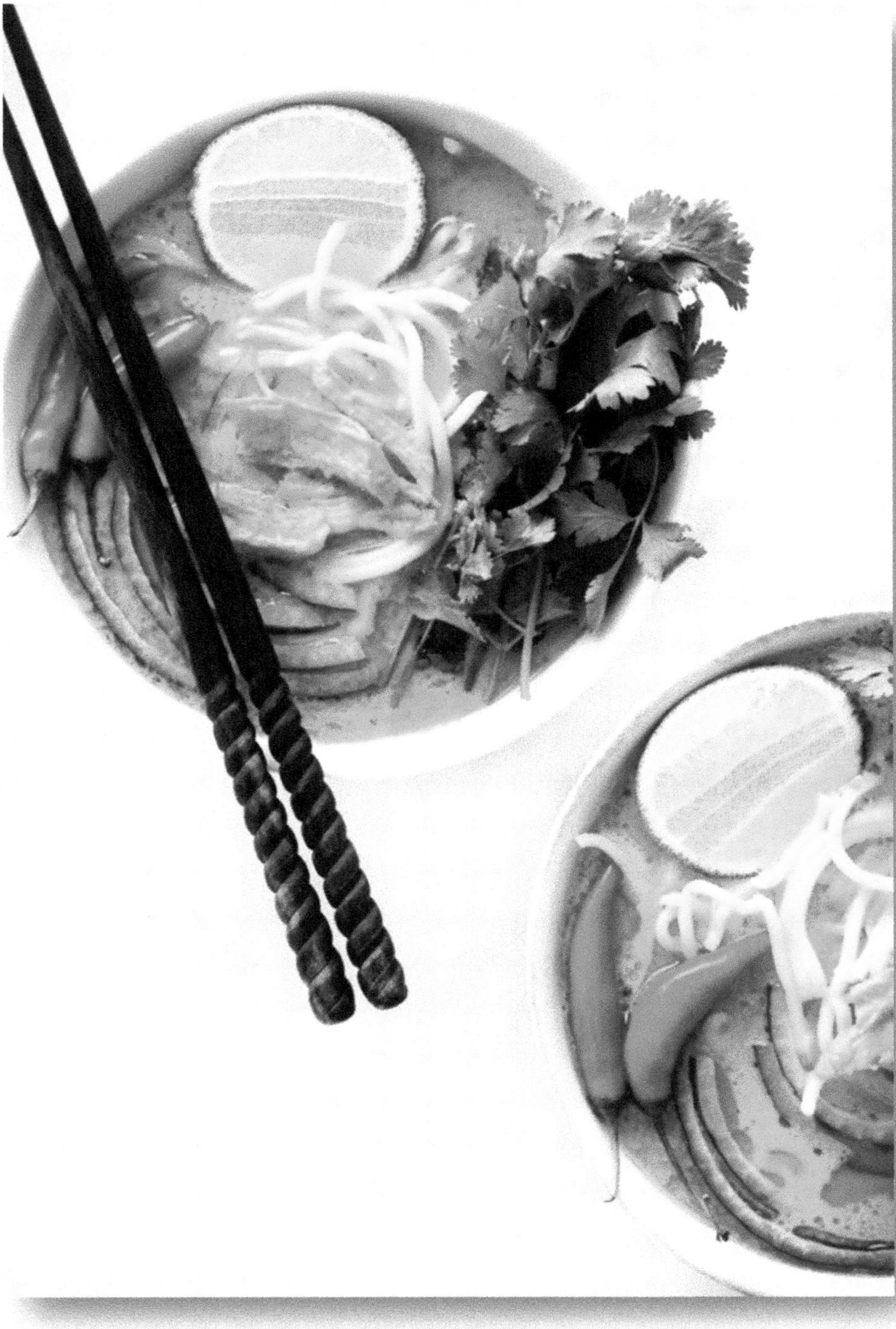

Collard Green Pasta

Preparation Time: 10 minutes

Cooking Time: 20 minutes

Servings: 4

Ingredients

- 2 tablespoons olive oil

- 4 garlic cloves, minced

- 8 oz. whole wheat pasta

- ½ cup panko bread crumbs

- 1 tablespoon nutritional yeast

- 1 teaspoon red pepper flakes

- 1 large bunch collard greens

- 1 large lemon, zest and juiced

Directions:

1. Fill a suitable pot with salted water and boil it on high heat.

2. Add pasta to the boiling water and cook until it is al dente, then rinse under cold water.

3. Reserve ½ cup of the cooking liquid from the pasta.

4. Place a non-stick pan over medium heat and add 1 tablespoon olive oil.

5. Stir in half of the garlic, then sauté for 30 seconds.

6. Add breadcrumbs and sauté for approximately 5 minutes.

7. Toss in red pepper flakes and nutritional yeast then mix well.

8. Transfer the breadcrumbs mixture to a plate and clean the pan.

9. Add the remaining tablespoon oil to the nonstick pan.

10. Stir in the garlic clove, salt, black pepper, and chard leaves.

11. Cook for 5 minutes until the leaves are wilted.

12. Add pasta along with the reserved pasta liquid.

13. Mix well, then add garlic crumbs, lemon juice, and zest.

14. Toss well, then serve warm.

Nutrition: Calories: 45Fat: 2.5gProtein: 4gCarbohydrates: 9gFiber: 4gSugar: 3gSodium: 20mg

Glazed Avocado

Preparation Time: 10 minutes

Cooking Time: 12 minutes

Servings: 4

Ingredients:

- 1 tablespoon stevia

- 1 teaspoon olive oil

- 1 teaspoon water

- 1 teaspoon lemon juice

- ½ teaspoon rosemary, dried

- ½ teaspoon ground black pepper

- 2 avocados, peeled, pitted and cut into large pieces

Directions:

1. Heat up a pan with the oil over medium heat, add the avocados, stevia and the other ingredients, toss, cook for 12 minutes, divide into bowls and serve.

Nutrition: Calories 262 Fat 9.6 Fiber 0.1 Carbs 6.5 Protein 7.9

Mango and Leeks Meatballs

Preparation Time: 20 minutes

Cooking Time: 10 minutes

Servings: 4

Ingredients:

- 1 tablespoon mango puree

- 1 cup leeks, chopped

- ½ cup tofu, crumbled

- 1 teaspoon dried oregano

- 1 tablespoon almond flour

- 1 teaspoon olive oil

- 1 tablespoon flax meal

- ½ teaspoon chili flakes

Directions:

1. In the mixing bowl, mix up mango puree with leeks, tofu and the other ingredients except the oil and stir well.

2. Make the small meatballs.

3. After this, pour the olive oil in the skillet and heat it up.

4. Add the meatballs in the skillet and cook them for 4 minutes from each side.

Nutrition: Calories 147 Fat 8.6 Fiber 4.5 Carbs 5.6 Protein 5.3

STIR-FRIED, GRILLED VEGETABLES

Grilled Avocado Guacamole

Preparation Time: 10 minutes

Cooking Time: 20 minutes

Servings: 4

Ingredients:

- ½ teaspoon olive oil
- 1 lime, halved
- ½ onion, halved
- 1 serrano chile, halved, stemmed, and seeded
- 3 Haas avocados, skin on
- 2–3 tablespoons fresh cilantro, chopped
- ½ teaspoon smoked salt

Directions:

1. Preheat the grill over medium heat.
2. Brush the grilling grates with olive oil and place chile, onion, and lime on it.
3. Grill the onion for 10 minutes, chile for 5 minutes, and lime for 2 minutes.
4. Transfer the veggies to a large bowl.
5. Now cut the avocados in half and grill them for 5 minutes.
6. Mash the flesh of the grilled avocado in a bowl.
7. Chop the other grilled veggies and add them to the avocado mash.
8. Stir in remaining ingredients and mix well.
9. Serve.

Nutrition: Calories: 165 Total Fat: 17g Carbs: 4g Net Carbs: 2g Fiber: 1g Protein: 1g

Tofu Hoagie Rolls

Preparation Time: 10 minutes

Cooking Time: 20 minutes

Servings: 6

Ingredients:

- ½ cup vegetable broth

- ¼ cup hot sauce

- 1 tablespoon vegan butter

- 1 (16 ounce) package tofu, pressed and diced

- 4 cups cabbage, shredded

- 2 medium apples, grated

- 1 medium shallot, grated

- 6 tablespoons vegan mayonnaise

- 1 tablespoon apple cider vinegar

- Salt and black pepper

- 4 6-inch hoagie rolls, toasted

Directions:

1. In a saucepan, combine broth with butter and hot sauce and bring to a boil.

2. Add tofu and reduce the heat to a simmer.

3. Cook for 10 minutes then remove from heat and let sit for 10 minutes to marinate.

4. Toss cabbage and rest of the ingredients in a salad bowl.

5. Prepare and set up a grill on medium heat.

6. Drain the tofu and grill for 5 minutes per side.

7. Lay out the toasted hoagie rolls and add grilled tofu to each hoagie

8. Add the cabbage mixture evenly between them then close it.

9. Serve.

Nutrition: Calories: 111 Total Fat: 11g Carbs: 5g Net Carbs: 1g Fiber: 0g Protein: 1g

DIP AND SPREAD RECIPES

Crunchy Peanut Butter Apple Dip

Preparation Time: 10 minutes

Cooking Time: 10 minutes

Servings: 2

Ingredients:

- 1 carton (8 oz.) reduced-fat spreadable cream cheese

- 1 cup creamy peanut butter

- 1/4 cup coconut milk

- 1 tablespoon brown sugar

- 1 teaspoon vanilla extract

- 1/2 cup chopped unsalted peanuts

- Apple slices

Directions:

1. Beat the initial 5 ingredients in a small bowl until combined. Mix in peanuts. Serve with slices of apple, then put the leftovers in the fridge.

Nutrition: Calories 125 Fat 5 Carbs 23 Protein 9

Creamy Cucumber Yogurt Dip

Preparation Time: 15 minutes

Cooking Time: 15 minutes

Servings: 4

Ingredients:

- 1 cup (8 oz.) reduced-fat plain yogurt

- 4 oz. reduced-fat cream cheese

- 1/2 cup chopped seeded peeled cucumber

- 1-1/2 teaspoon. finely chopped onion

- 1-1/2 teaspoon. snipped fresh dill or 1/2 teaspoon dill weed

- 1 teaspoon lemon juice

- 1 teaspoon grated lemon peel

- 1 garlic clove, minced

- 1/4 teaspoon salt

- 1/4 teaspoon pepper

- Assorted fresh vegetables

Directions:

1. Mix the cream cheese and yogurt in a small bowl. Stir in pepper, salt, garlic, peel, lemon juice, dill, onion, and cucumber. Put on the cover and let it chill in the fridge. Serve it with the veggies.

Nutrition: Calories 55 Fat 4 Carbs 12 Protein 6

PASTA & NOODLES

Creamy Vegan Mushroom Pasta

Preparation Time: 10 minutes

Cooking Time: 30 minutes

Servings: 6

Ingredients:

- 2 cups frozen peas, thawed

- 3 tablespoons flour, unbleached

- 3 cups almond breeze, unsweetened

- 1 tablespoon nutritional yeast

- 1/3 cup fresh parsley, chopped, plus extra for garnish

- ¼ cup olive oil

- 1 pound pasta of choice

- 4 cloves garlic, minced

- 2/3 cup shallots, chopped

- 8 cups mixed mushrooms, sliced

- Salt and black pepper, to taste

Directions:

1. Take a bowl and boil pasta in salted water.

2. Heat olive oil in a pan over medium heat.

3. Add mushrooms, garlic, shallots and ½ tsp salt and cook for 15 minutes.

4. Sprinkle flour on the vegetables and stir for a minute while cooking.

5. Add almond beverage, stir constantly.

6. Let it simmer for 5 minutes and add pepper to it.

7. Cook for 3 more minutes and remove from heat.

8. Stir in nutritional yeast.

9. Add peas, salt, and pepper.

10. Cook for another minute and add

11. Add pasta to this sauce.

12. Garnish and serve!

Nutrition: Calories: 364 Total Fat: 28g Protein: 24g Total Carbs: 4g Fiber: 2g Net Carbs: 2g

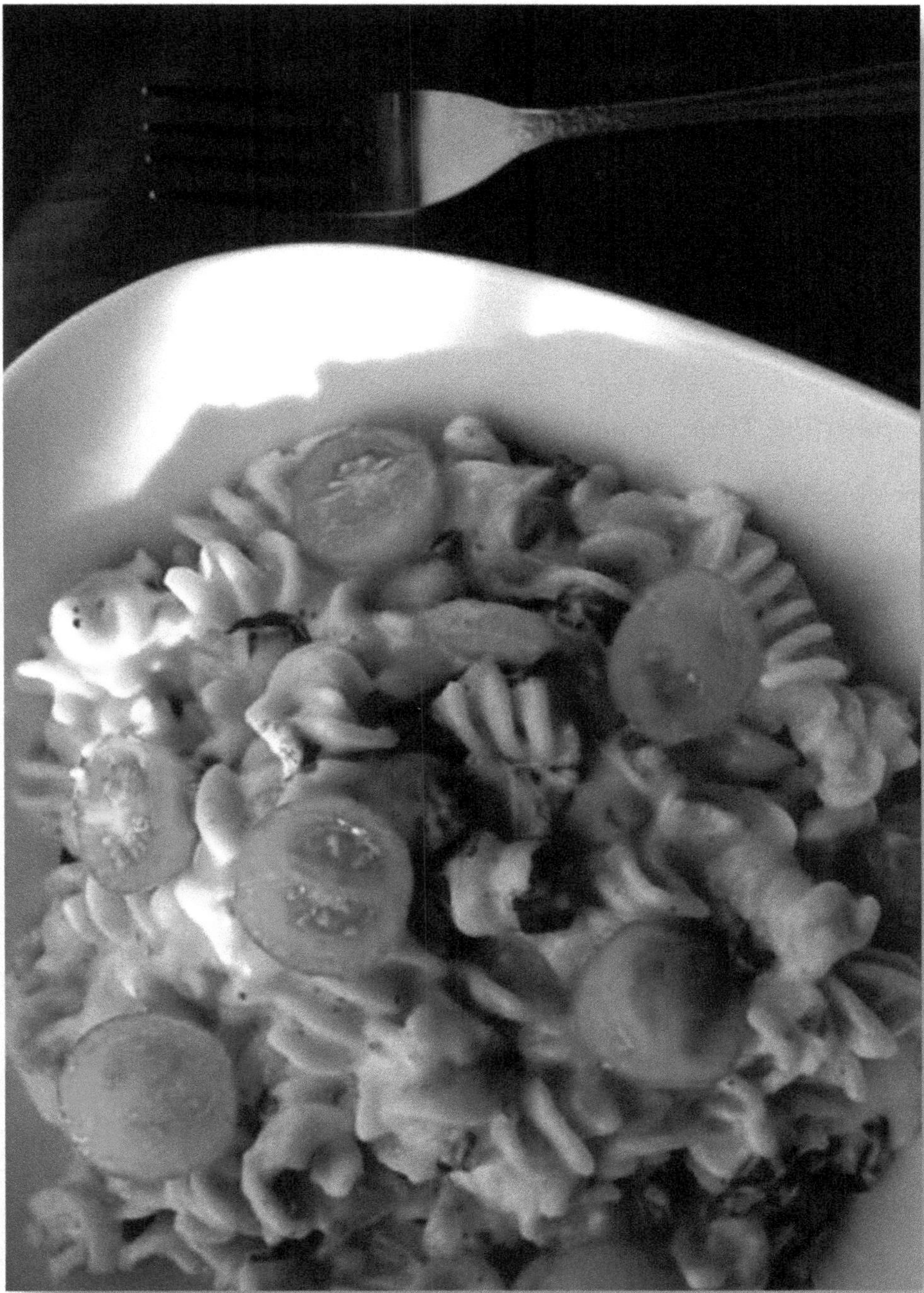

SIDE DISHES

Paprika Sweet Potato

Preparation Time: 10 minutes

Cooking Time: 11 minutes

Servings: 2

Ingredients:

- 2 sweet potatoes

- 2 teaspoons sweet paprika

- 1/2 teaspoon oregano, dried

- 1 teaspoon chili powder

- 1 teaspoon chives, chopped

- 1/2 cup of water

Directions:

1. Pour water in the instant pot and insert steamer rack.

2. Put potatoes on the rack and close the lid.

3. Set Manual mode (High pressure) and cook for 11 minutes. Then use quick pressure release.

4. Transfer the potatoes on the plate, cut into halves, sprinkle the rest of the Ingredients on top and serve.

Nutrition: Calories: 159, Fat: 3.4, Fiber: 2.8, Carbs: 33.8, Protein: 3.6

Wild Rice and Corn

Preparation Time: 10 minutes

Cooking Time: 8 minutes

Servings: 4

Ingredients:

- 1 cup wild rice

- 1 tablespoon Italian seasoning

- 1/4 cup corn kernels, canned

- 1 teaspoon chili powder

- 1 teaspoon salt

- 2 cups vegetable broth

- 1 tablespoon chives, chopped

- 2 tablespoons olive oil

Directions:

1. Pour olive oil in the instant pot and set Saute mode.

2. Add rice and seasoning and cook for 2 minutes.

3. Add the rest of the Ingredients and toss.

4. Set Manual mode (High pressure) and close the lid. Seal it.

5. Cook rice for 6 minutes. Use quick pressure release.

Nutrition: Calories: 254 Fat: 4.3 Fiber: 1.5 Carbs: 25.4 Protein: 5.4

Kale Polenta

Preparation Time: 5 minutes

Cooking Time: 8 minutes

Servings: 5

Ingredients:

- 1 cup polenta

- 1/2 cup kale, chopped

- 1 teaspoon turmeric powder

- 1 teaspoon smoked paprika

- 4 cups vegetable broth

- 2 tablespoons coconut milk

- 1/2 teaspoon ground black pepper

- 1 teaspoon salt

Directions:

1. Whisk together polenta and vegetable broth.

2. Pour mixture in the instant pot, add the rest of the Ingredients and toss.

3. Close the lid and cook it on Manual mode (High pressure) for 8 minutes. Use quick pressure release/

4. Transfer cooked polenta in the bowl, stir and serve.

Nutrition: Calories: 182, Fat: 2.8, Fiber: 1, Carbs: 20.5, Protein: 6.3

SOUP AND STEW

Tomato Gazpacho

Preparation Time: 30 minutes

Cooking Time: 55 minutes

Servings: 6

Ingredients:

- 2 Tablespoons + 1 Teaspoon Red Wine Vinegar, Divided
- ½ Teaspoon Pepper
- 1 Teaspoon Sea Salt
- 1 Avocado,
- ¼ Cup Basil, Fresh & Chopped
- 3 Tablespoons + 2 Teaspoons Olive Oil, Divided
- 1 Clove Garlic, crushed
- 1 Red Bell Pepper, Sliced & Seeded
- 1 Cucumber, Chunked
- 2 ½ lbs. Large Tomatoes, Cored & Chopped

Directions:

1. Place half of your cucumber, bell pepper, and ¼ cup of each tomato in a bowl, covering. Set it in the fried.

2. Puree your remaining tomatoes, cucumber and bell pepper with garlic, three tablespoons oil, two tablespoons of vinegar, sea salt and black pepper into a blender, blending until smooth. Transfer it to a bowl, and chill for two hours.

3. Chop the avocado, adding it to your chopped vegetables, adding your remaining oil, vinegar, salt, pepper and basil.

4. Ladle your tomato puree mixture into bowls, and serve with chopped vegetables as a salad.

5. Interesting Facts:

6. Avocados themselves are ranked within the top five of the healthiest foods on the planet, so you know that the oil that is produced from them is too. It is loaded with healthy fats and essential fatty acids. Like race bran oil it is perfect to cook with as well! Bonus: Helps in the prevention of diabetes and lowers cholesterol levels.

Nutrition: Calories 201 Protein 23g Fat 4 Carbs 2

Tomato Pumpkin Soup

Preparation Time: 25 minutes

Cooking Time: 25 minutes

Servings: 4

Ingredients:

- 2 cups pumpkin, diced
- 1/2 cup tomato, chopped
- 1/2 cup onion, chopped
- 1 1/2 tsp curry powder
- 1/2 tsp paprika
- 2 cups vegetable stock
- 1 tsp olive oil
- 1/2 tsp garlic, minced

Directions:

1. In a saucepan, add oil, garlic, and onion and sauté for 3 minutes over medium heat.

2. Add remaining ingredients into the saucepan and bring to boil.

3. Reduce heat and cover and simmer for 10 minutes.

4. Puree the soup using a blender until smooth.

5. Stir well and serve warm.

Nutrition: Calories: 340 Protein: 50 g Carbohydrate: 14 g Fat: 10g

Creamy Garlic Onion Soup

Preparation Time: 45 minutes

Cooking Time: 25 minutes

Servings: 4

Ingredients:

- 1 onion, sliced

- 4 cups vegetable stock

- 1 1/2 tbsp. olive oil

- 1 shallot, sliced

- 2 garlic clove, chopped

- 1 leek, sliced

- Salt

Directions:

1. Add stock and olive oil in a saucepan and bring to boil.

2. Add remaining ingredients and stir well.

3. Cover and simmer for 25 minutes.

4. Puree the soup using an immersion blender until smooth.

5. Stir well and serve warm.

Nutrition: Calories 115 Protein 30g Fat 0 Carbs 3

Green Spinach Kale Soup

Preparation Time: 10 minutes

Cooking Time: 5 minutes

Servings: 6

Ingredients:

- 2 avocados
- 8 oz. spinach
- 8 oz. kale
- 1 fresh lime juice
- 1 cup water
- 3 1/3 cup coconut milk
- 3 oz. olive oil
- 1/4 tsp pepper
- 1 tsp salt

Directions:

1. Heat olive oil in a saucepan over medium heat.

2. Add kale and spinach to the saucepan and sauté for 2-3 minutes. Remove saucepan from heat. Add coconut milk, spices, avocado, and water. Stir well.

3. Puree the soup using an immersion blender until smooth and creamy. Add fresh lime juice and stir well.

4. Serve and enjoy.

Nutrition: Calories: 312 Protein: 9g Fat: 10 Carbs: 22

Cabbage & Beet Stew

Preparation Time: 20 minutes

Cooking Time: 10 minutes

Servings: 4

Ingredients:

- 2 Tablespoons Olive Oil

- 3 Cups Vegetable Broth

- 2 Tablespoons Lemon Juice, Fresh

- ½ Teaspoon Garlic Powder

- ½ Cup Carrots, Shredded

- 2 Cups Cabbage, Shredded

- 1 Cup Beets, Shredded

- Dill for Garnish

- ½ Teaspoon Onion Powder

- Sea Salt & Black Pepper to Taste

Directions:

1. Heat oil in a pot, and then sauté your vegetables.

2. Pour your broth in, mixing in your seasoning. Simmer until it's cooked through, and then top with dill.

Nutrition: Kcal: 263 Carbohydrates: 8 g Protein: 20.3 g Fat: 24 g

Basil Tomato Soup

Preparation Time: 10 minutes

Cooking Time: 10 minutes

Servings: 6

Ingredients:

- 28 oz. can tomatoes
- ¼ cup basil pesto
- ¼ tsp dried basil leaves
- 1 tsp apple cider vinegar
- 2 tbsp. erythritol
- ¼ tsp garlic powder
- ½ tsp onion powder
- 2 cups water
- 1 ½ tsp kosher salt

Directions:

1. Add tomatoes, garlic powder, onion powder, water, and salt in a saucepan.

2. Bring to boil over medium heat. Reduce heat and simmer for 2 minutes.

3. Remove saucepan from heat and puree the soup using a blender until smooth.

4. Stir in pesto, dried basil, vinegar, and erythritol.

5. Stir well and serve warm.

Nutrition: Kcal: 662 Carbohydrates: 18 g Protein: 8 g Fat: 55 g

SMOOTHIES AND BEVERAGES

Light Ginger Tea

Preparation Time: 5 minutes

Cooking Time: 10 to 15 minutes

Servings: 2

Ingredients:

- 1 small ginger knob, sliced into four 1-inch chunks

- 4 cups water

- Juice of 1 large lemon

- Maple syrup, to taste

Directions:

1. Add the ginger knob and water in a saucepan, then simmer over medium heat for 10 to 15 minutes.

2. Turn off the heat, then mix in the lemon juice. Strain the liquid to remove the ginger, then fold in the maple syrup and serve.

Nutrition: Calories: 32 Fat: 0.1g Carbs: 8.6g Fiber: 0.1g Protein: 0.1g

Lime and Cucumber Electrolyte Drink

Preparation Time: 5 minutes

Cooking Time: 0 minutes

Servings: 4

Ingredients:

- ¼ cup chopped cucumber

- 1 tablespoon fresh lime juice

- 1 tablespoon apple cider vinegar

- 2 tablespoons maple syrup

- ¼ teaspoon sea salt, optional

- 4 cups water

Directions:

1. Combine all the ingredients in a glass. Stir to mix well.

2. Refrigerate overnight before serving.

Nutrition: Calories: 114 Fat: 0.1g Carbs: 28.9g Fiber: 0.3g Protein: 0.3g

BREAD RECIPES

Beer Bread

Preparation Time: 10-15 minutes

Cooking Time: 2.5-3 hours

Serving Size: 2 ounces (56.7g)

Ingredients:

- 3 cups bread flour

- Two tablespoons sugar

- Two ¼ teaspoons yeast

- 1 ½ teaspoons salt

- 2/3 cup beer

- 1/3 cup water

- Two tablespoons vegetable oil

Direction:

1. Add all ingredients into a pan in this order: water, beer, oil, salt, sugar, flour, and yeast.

2. Start the bread machine with the "Basic" or "Normal" mode on and light to medium crust colour.

3. Let the machine complete all cycles.

4. Take out the pan from the machine.

5. Transfer the beer bread into a wire rack to cool it down for about an hour.

6. Cut into 12 slices, and serve.

Nutrition: Calories: 130 | Carbohydrates: 25g Fat: 1g | Protein: 4g

Onion and Mushroom Bread

Preparation Time: 10 minutes

Cooking Time: 1 hour

Serving Size: 2 ounces (56.7g)

Ingredients:

- 4 ounces mushrooms, chopped

- 4 cups bread flour

- Three tablespoons sugar

- Four teaspoons fast-acting yeast

- Four teaspoons dried onions, minced

- 1 ½ teaspoons salt

- ½ teaspoon garlic powder

- ¾ cup of water

Direction:

1. Pour the water first into the bread pan, and then add all of the dry ingredients.

2. Press the "Fast" cycle mode of the bread machine.

3. Wait until all cycles are completed.

4. Transfer the bread from the pan into a wire rack.

5. Wait for one hour before slicing the bread into 12 pieces.

6. Serving Size: 2 ounces per slice

Nutrition: Calories: 120 | Carbohydrates: 25g Fat: 0g | Protein: 5g

Low-Carb Multigrain Bread

Preparation Time: 15 minutes

Cooking Time: 1.5 hours

Serving Size: 1 ounce (28.3g)

Ingredients:

- ¾ cup whole-wheat flour

- ¼ cup cornmeal

- ¼ cup oatmeal

- Two tablespoons 7-grain cereals

- Two tablespoons baking powder

- One teaspoon salt

- ¼ teaspoon baking soda

- ¾ cup of water

- ¼ cup of vegetable oil

- ¼ cup of orange juice

- Three tablespoons aquafaba

Direction:

1. In the bread pan, add the wet ingredients first, then the dry ingredients.

2. Press the "Quick" or "Cake" mode of your bread machine.

3. Wait until all cycles are through.

4. Remove the bread pan from the machine.

5. Let the bread rest for 10 minutes in the pan before taking it out to cool down further.

6. Slice the bread after an hour has passed.

Nutrition: Calories: 60 | Carbohydrates: 9g Fat: 2g | Protein: 1g

SAUCES, DRESSINGS, AND DIPS

Homemade Tzatziki Sauce

Preparation Time: 20 minutes

Cooking Time: 0 minutes

Servings: 1

Ingredients:

- 2 ounces (57 g) raw, unsalted cashews (about ½ cup)

- 2 tablespoons lemon juice

- 1/3 cup water

- 1 small clove garlic

- 1 cup chopped cucumber, peeled

- 2 tablespoons fresh dill

Directions:

1. In a blender, add the cashews, lemon juice, water, and garlic. Keep it aside for at least 15 minutes to soften the cashews.

2. Blend the ingredients until smooth. Stir in the chopped cucumber and dill, and continue to blend until it reaches your desired consistency. It doesn't need to be totally smooth. Feel free to add more water if you like a thinner consistency.

3. Transfer to an airtight container and chill for at least 30 minutes for best flavors.

4. Bring the sauce to room temperature and shake well before serving.

Nutrition: Calories: 208 Fat: 13.5g Carbs: 15.0 g Protein: 6.7g Fiber: 2.8g

SALADS RECIPES

Lentil, Lemon & Mushroom Salad

Preparation Time: 10 minutes

Cooking Time: 0 minutes

Servings: 2

Ingredients:

- ½ cup dry lentils of choice

- 2 cups vegetable broth

- 3 cups mushrooms, thickly sliced

- 1 cup sweet or purple onion, chopped

- 4 tsp. extra virgin olive oil

- 2 tbsp. garlic powder

- ¼ tsp. chili flakes

- 1 tbsp. lemon juice

- 2 tbsp. cilantro, chopped

- ½ cup arugula

- ¼ tsp Salt

- ¼ tsp pepper

Directions:

1. Sprout the lentils according the method. (Don't cook them).

2. Place the vegetable stock in a deep saucepan and bring it to a boil.

3. Add the lentils to the boiling broth, cover the pan, and cook for about 5 minutes over low heat until the lentils are a bit tender.

4. Remove the pan from heat and drain the excess water.

5. Put a frying pan over high heat and add 2 tablespoons of olive oil.

6. Add the onions, garlic, and chili flakes, and cook until the onions are almost translucent, around 5 to 10 minutes while stirring.

7. Add the mushrooms to the frying pan and mix in thoroughly. Continue cooking until the onions are completely translucent and the mushrooms have softened; remove the pan from the heat.

8. Mix the lentils, onions, mushrooms, and garlic in a large bowl.

9. Add the lemon juice and the remaining olive oil. Toss or stir to combine everything thoroughly.

10. Serve the mushroom/onion mixture over some arugala in bowl, adding salt and pepper to taste, or, store and enjoy later!

Nutrition: Calories 365 Total Fat 11.7g Saturated Fat 1.9g Cholesterol 0mg Sodium 1071mg Total Carbohydrate 45.2g Dietary Fiber 18g Total Sugars 8.2g Protein 22.8g Vitamin D 378mcg Calcium 67mg Iron 8mg Potassium 1212mg

FRUIT SALAD RECIPES

Fruit Salad with Sweet Lime Dressing

Preparation Time: 15 Minutes

Cooking Time: 0 Minutes

Servings: 9

Ingredients:

Salad

- Mint, fresh chopped, one cup

- Lime juice, two tablespoons

- Kiwi, five, peeled and sliced

- Mangoes, two, peeled and chopped

- Green grapes, one cup cut in half

- Blackberries, one cup

- Blueberries, one cup

- Strawberries, one cup sliced

Sweet Lime Dressing

- Powdered sugar, two tablespoons

- Lime juice, two tablespoons

Directions:

1. Mix together until smooth in a small-sized bowl the powdered sugar and the lime juice.

2. Mix together in a large-sized bowl the fruits, then pour on the dressing and gently toss all of the fruits together well to coat all of the pieces.

3. This will stay good in the refrigerator for no more than one day.

Nutrition: Calories: 50 Protein: 1g Fat: 1g Carbs: 12g

ENTRÉES

Quick and Easy Curry

Preparation Time: 10 minutes

Cooking Time: 25 minutes

Servings: 4

Ingredients:

- Bell peppers, red, thinly sliced – 2

- Chickpeas, cooked, liquid drained off – 2.5 cups or a 19 ounce can

- Broccoli florets, roughly chopped – 4 cups

- Onion, diced – 1

- Light coconut milk – 14 ounces

- Maple syrup – 1 teaspoon

- Sea salt – 1 teaspoon

- Tamari sauce – 1 tablespoon

- Garlic, minced – 4 cloves

- Cumin – 1 tablespoon

- Curry powder – 1 tablespoon

- Black pepper, ground - .25 teaspoon

- Water - .25 cup

Directions:

1. Place all of the vegetables and the water into a large non-stick skillet and allow them to cook together over a temperature of medium-high heat for three minutes.

2. Add the remaining ingredients and continue to cook the curry for seven to eight minutes, until the vegetables are tender but still have a little bite. You don't want to overcook the vegetables until they become mush, as they are best with their texture intact.

3. Remove the curry from the heat, give it a good stir, and serve it with your favorite cooked grains or pasta.

Nutrition: Number of Calories in Individual **Servings:** 342 Protein Grams: 15 Fat Grams: 6 Total Carbohydrates Grams: 52 Net Carbohydrates Grams: 39

GRAINS AND BEANS

Brown Rice with Mushrooms

Preparation Time: 15 minutes

Cooking Time: 20 minutes

Servings: 6 to 8

Ingredients:

- ½ pound (227 g) mushrooms, sliced

- 1 green bell pepper, chopped

- 1 onion, chopped

- 1 bunch scallions, chopped

- 2 cloves garlic, minced

- ½ cup water

- 5 cups cooked brown rice

- 1 (16-ounce / 454-g) can chopped tomatoes

- 1 (4-ounce / 113-g) can chopped green chilies

- 2 teaspoons chili powder

- 1 teaspoon ground cumin

Directions:

1. In a large pot, sauté the mushrooms, green pepper, onion, scallions, and garlic in the water for 10 minutes.

2. Stir in the remaining ingredients. Cook over low heat for about 10 minutes, or until heated through, stirring frequently.

3. Serve immediately.

Nutrition: Calories: 185 Fat: 2.6g Carbs: 34.5g Protein: 6.1g Fiber: 4.3g

DRINKS

Warm Spiced Lemon Drink

Preparation Time: 10 minutes

Cooking Time: 2 hours

Servings: 12

Ingredients:

- 1 cinnamon stick, about 3 inches long

- 1/2 teaspoon of whole cloves

- 2 cups of coconut sugar

- 4 fluid of ounce pineapple juice

- 1/2 cup and 2 tablespoons of lemon juice

- 12 fluid ounce of orange juice

- 2 1/2 quarts of water

Directions:

1. Pour water into a 6-quarts slow cooker and stir the sugar and lemon juice properly.

2. Wrap the cinnamon, the whole cloves in cheesecloth and tie its corners with string.

3. Immerse this cheesecloth bag in the liquid present in the slow cooker and cover it with the lid.

4. Then plug in the slow cooker and let it cook on high heat setting for 2 hours or until it is heated thoroughly.

5. When done, discard the cheesecloth bag and serve the drink hot or cold.

Nutrition: Calories 523 Carbohydrates: 4.6g Protein: 47.9g Fat: 34.8g

Banana Weight Loss Juice

Preparation Time: 10 Minutes

Cooking Time: 0 Minutes

Servings: 1

Ingredients:

- Water (1/3 C.)

- Apple (1, Sliced)

- Orange (1, Sliced)

- Banana (1, Sliced)

- Lemon Juice (1 T.)

Directions:

1. Looking to boost your weight loss? The key is taking in less calories; this recipe can get you there.

2. Simply place everything into your blender, blend on high for twenty seconds, and then pour into your glass.

Nutrition: Calories: 289 Total Carbohydrate: 2 g Cholesterol: 3 mg Total Fat: 17 g Fiber: 2 g Protein: 7 g Sodium: 163 mg

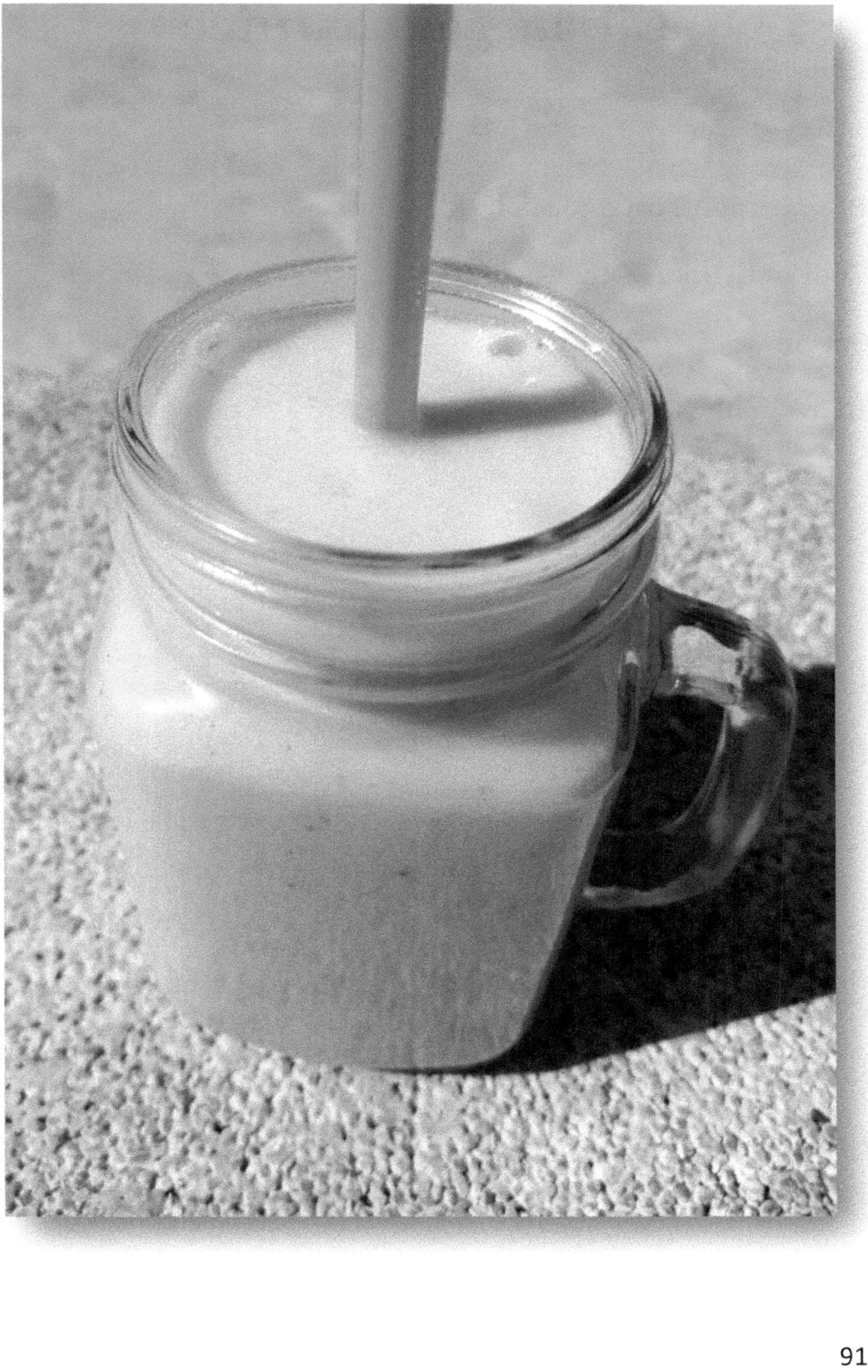

Citrus Detox Juice

Preparation Time: 10 Minutes

Cooking Time: 0 Minutes

Servings: 4

Ingredients:

- Water (3 C.)

- Lemon (1, Sliced)

- Grapefruit (1, Sliced)

- Orange (1, Sliced)

Directions:

1. While starting your new diet, it is going to be vital to stay hydrated. This detox juice is the perfect solution and offers some extra flavor.

2. Begin by peeling and slicing up your fruit. Once this is done, place in a pitcher of water and infuse the water overnight.

Nutrition: Calories: 269 Total Carbohydrate: 2 g Cholesterol: 3 mg Total Fat: 14 g Fiber: 2 g Protein: 7 g Sodium: 183 mg

Stress Relief Detox Drink

Preparation Time: 5 Minutes

Cooking Time: 0 Minutes

Servings: 1

Ingredients:

- Water (1 Pitcher)

- Mint

- Lemon (1, Sliced)

- Basil

- Strawberries (1 C., Sliced)

- Ice

Directions:

1. Life can be a pretty stressful event. Luckily, there is water to help keep you cool, calm, and collected! The lemon works like an energizer, the basil is a natural antidepressant, and mint can help your stomach do its job better. As for the strawberries, those are just for some sweetness!

2. When you are ready, take all of the ingredients and place into a pitcher of water overnight and enjoy the next day.

Nutrition: Calories: 189 Total Carbohydrate: 2 g Cholesterol: 73 mg
Total Fat: 17 g Fiber: 0 g Protein: 7 g Sodium: 163 mg

DESERTS

Almond Butter, Oat and Protein Energy Balls

Preparation Time: 1 hour and 10 minutes

Cooking Time: 3 minutes

Servings: 4

Ingredients:

- 1 cup rolled oats

- ½ cup honey

- 2 ½ scoops of vanilla protein powder

- 1 cup almond butter

- Chia seeds for rolling

Directions:

1. Take a skillet pan, place it over medium heat, add butter and honey, stir and cook for 2 minutes until warm.

2. Transfer the mixture into a bowl, stir in protein powder until mixed, and then stir in oatmeal until combined.

3. Shape the mixture into balls, roll them into chia seeds, then arrange them on a cookie sheet and refrigerate for 1 hour until firm.

4. Serve straight away

Nutrition: Calories: 200 Cal Fat: 10 g Carbs: 21 g Protein: 7 g Fiber: 4 g

Chocolate and Avocado Truffles

Preparation Time: 1 hour and 10 minutes

Cooking Time: 1 minute

Servings: 18

Ingredients:

- 1 medium avocado, ripe

- 2 tablespoons cocoa powder

- 10 ounces of dark chocolate chips

Directions:

1. Scoop out the flesh from avocado, place it in a bowl, then mash with a fork until smooth, and stir in 1/2 cup chocolate chips.

2. Place remaining chocolate chips in a heatproof bowl and microwave for 1 minute until chocolate has melted, stirring halfway.

3. Add melted chocolate into avocado mixture, stir well until blended, and then refrigerate for 1 hour.

4. Then shape the mixture into balls, 1 tablespoon of mixture per ball, and roll in cocoa powder until covered.

5. Serve straight away.

Nutrition: Calories: 59 Cal Fat: 4 g Carbs: 7 g Protein: 0 g Fiber: 1 g

Coconut Oil Cookies

Preparation Time: 10 minutes

Cooking Time: 10 minutes

Servings: 15

Ingredients:

- 3 1/4 cup oats

- 1/2 teaspoons salt

- 2 cups coconut Sugar

- 1 teaspoons vanilla extract, unsweetened

- 1/4 cup cocoa powder

- 1/2 cup liquid Coconut Oil

- 1/2 cup peanut butter

- 1/2 cup cashew milk

Directions:

1. Take a saucepan, place it over medium heat, add all the ingredients except for oats and vanilla, stir until mixed, and then bring the mixture to boil.

2. Simmer the mixture for 4 minutes, mixing frequently, then remove the pan from heat and stir in vanilla.

3. Add oats, stir until well mixed and then scoop the mixture on a plate lined with wax paper.

4. Serve straight away.

Nutrition: Calories: 112 Cal Fat: 6.5 g Carbs: 13 g Protein: 1.4 g Fibe

r: 0.1

g

Apple Crumble

Preparation Time: 20 minutes

Cooking Time: 25 minutes

Servings: 6

Ingredients:

- For the filling

- 4 to 5 apples, cored and chopped (about 6 cups)

- ½ cup unsweetened applesauce, or ¼ cup water

- 2 to 3 tablespoons unrefined sugar (coconut, date, sucanat, maple syrup)

- 1 teaspoon ground cinnamon

- Pinch sea salt

- For the crumble

- 2 tablespoons almond butter, or cashew or sunflower seed butter

- 2 tablespoons maple syrup

- 1½ cups rolled oats

- ½ cup walnuts, finely chopped

- ½ teaspoon ground cinnamon

- 2 to 3 tablespoons unrefined granular sugar (coconut, date, sucanat)

Directions:

1. Preparing the Ingredients.

2. Preheat the oven to 350°F. Put the apples and applesauce in an 8-inch-square baking dish, and sprinkle with the sugar, cinnamon, and salt. Toss to combine.

3. In a medium bowl, mix together the nut butter and maple syrup until smooth and creamy. Add the oats, walnuts, cinnamon, and sugar and stir to coat, using your hands if necessary. (If you have a small food processor, pulse the oats and walnuts together before adding them to the mix.)

4. Sprinkle the topping over the apples, and put the dish in the oven.

5. Bake for 20 to 25 minutes, or until the fruit is soft and the topping is lightly browned.

Nutrition: Calories 195 Fat 7 g Carbohydrates 6 g Sugar 2 g Protein 24 g Cholesterol 65 mg

Seasoned Cinnamon Mango Popsicles

Preparation Time: 15 minutes

Cooking Time: 0 minute

Servings: 6

Ingredients:

- 1 1/2 cups of mango pulp
- 1 mango cut in cubes
- 1 cup brown sugar (packed)
- 2 Tbsp. lemon juice freshly squeezed
- 1 tsp cinnamon

- 1 pinch of salt

Directions:

1. Add all ingredients into your blender.

2. Blend until brown sugar dissolved.

3. Pour the mango mixture evenly in popsicle molds or cups.

4. Insert sticks into each mold.

5. Place molds in a freezer, and freeze for at least 5 to 6 hours.

6. Before serving, un-mold easy your popsicles placing molds under lukewarm water.

Nutrition: Calories: 423 Fat: 2g Fiber: 0g Carbs: 20g Protein: 33g

OTHER RECIPES

Lemony Romaine and Avocado Salad

Preparation Time: 15 minutes

Cooking Time: 0 minute

Servings: 6

Ingredients:

- 1 head romaine lettuce

- ½ cup pomegranate seeds

- ¼ cup pine nuts

- ¼ cup Lemon Vinaigrette

- 2 avocados

- Freshly ground black pepper

Directions:

2. Wash your vegetables and spin-dry then slice the leaves into bite-size pieces. Transfer the leaves in a large bowl, and toss with the pomegranate seeds, pine nuts, and half of the vinaigrette.

3. Slice the avocados in half. Remove the pit from each, and slice the avocados into long thin slices. Using a large spoon, carefully scoop the slices out of the peel.

4. Arrange your avocado slices on top of the lettuce in the bowl, and drizzle half of the remaining dressing over them. Carefully toss using your hands or a large metal spoon. Add the remaining dressing as needed.

5. Finish with a few sprinkles of pepper.

Nutrition: Calories: 217 Fat: 20g Carbs: 11g Protein 3g

Aloha Mango-Pineapple Smoothie

Preparation Time: 10 minutes

Cooking Time: 0 minute

Servings: 2

Ingredients:

- 1 large navel orange, peeled and quartered

- 1 cup frozen pineapple chunks

- 1 cup frozen mango chunks

- 1 tablespoon freshly squeezed lime juice

- ½ cup plain Greek yogurt

- ½ cup milk or coconut milk

- 1 tablespoon chia seeds (optional)

- 3 or 4 ice cubes

Directions:

1. Transfer all your ingredients in a blender and blend until smooth. If necessary, add additional milk or water to thin the smoothie to your preferred consistency.

Nutrition: Calories: 158 Fat: 1g Carbs: 35g Protein: 7g

Lightning Source UK Ltd.
Milton Keynes UK
UKHW020653100621
385265UK00005B/164

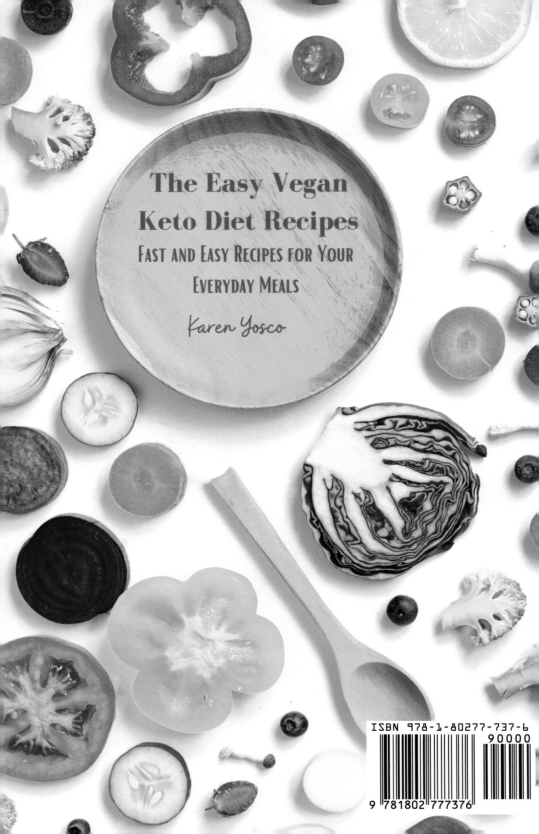

The Easy Vegan Keto Diet Recipes

Fast and Easy Recipes for Your Everyday Meals

Karen Yosco

ISBN 978-1-80277-737-6

90000

9 781802 777376

WHAT DO I DO WITH THIS?

1 minimalist minute

The **quick decision-making** method to get **time** in your life, **space** in your home and **save** money forever

Claudia Davide Montalto